NATIONAL GEOGRAPHIC

Our World Is Big

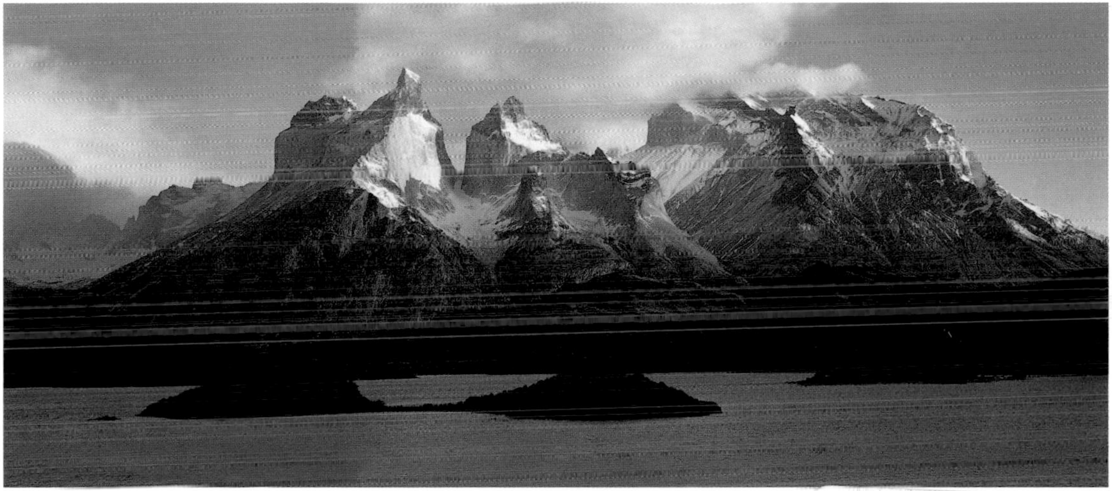

Liam Collins

T0052307

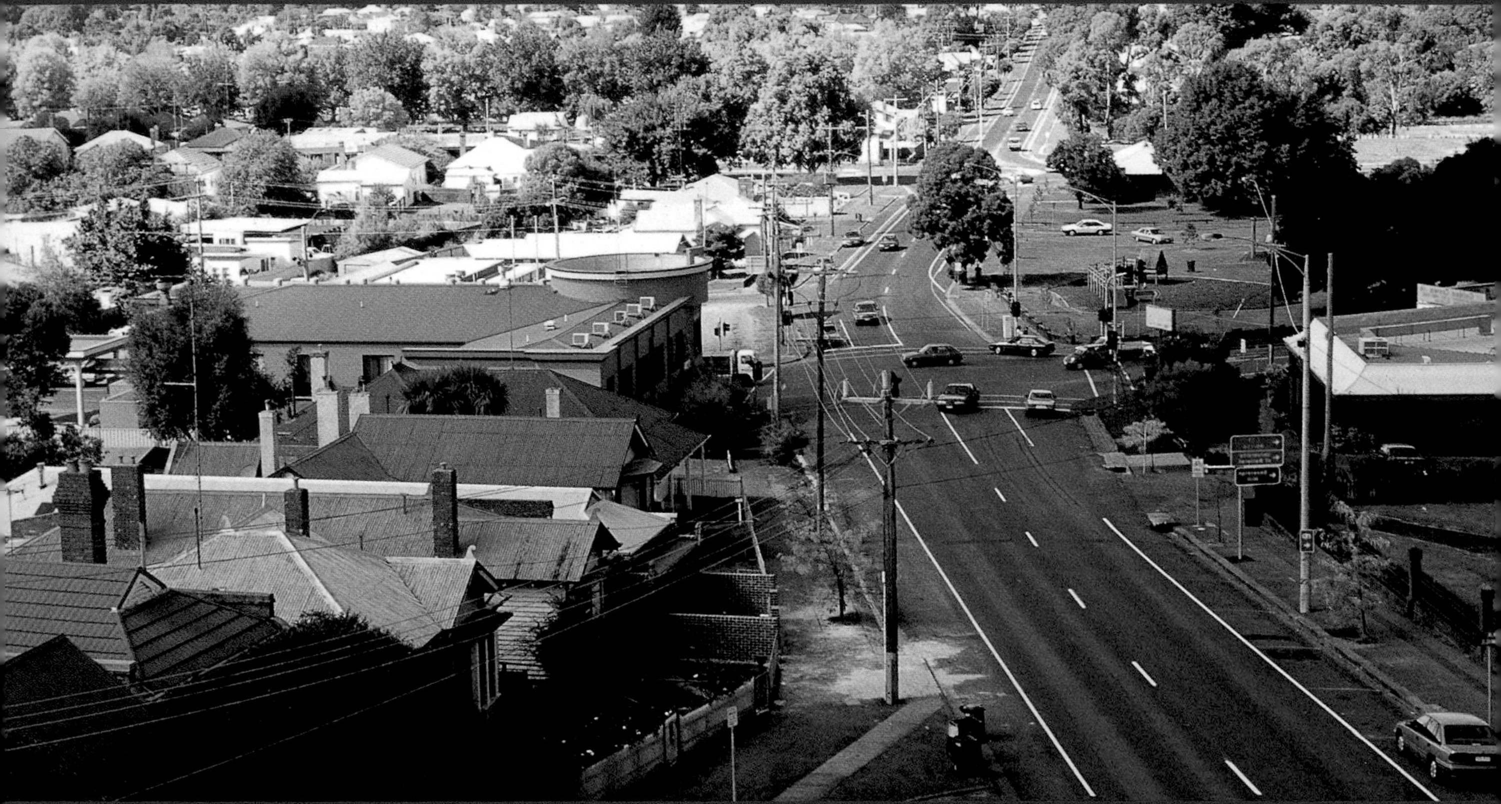

A town is **big**.

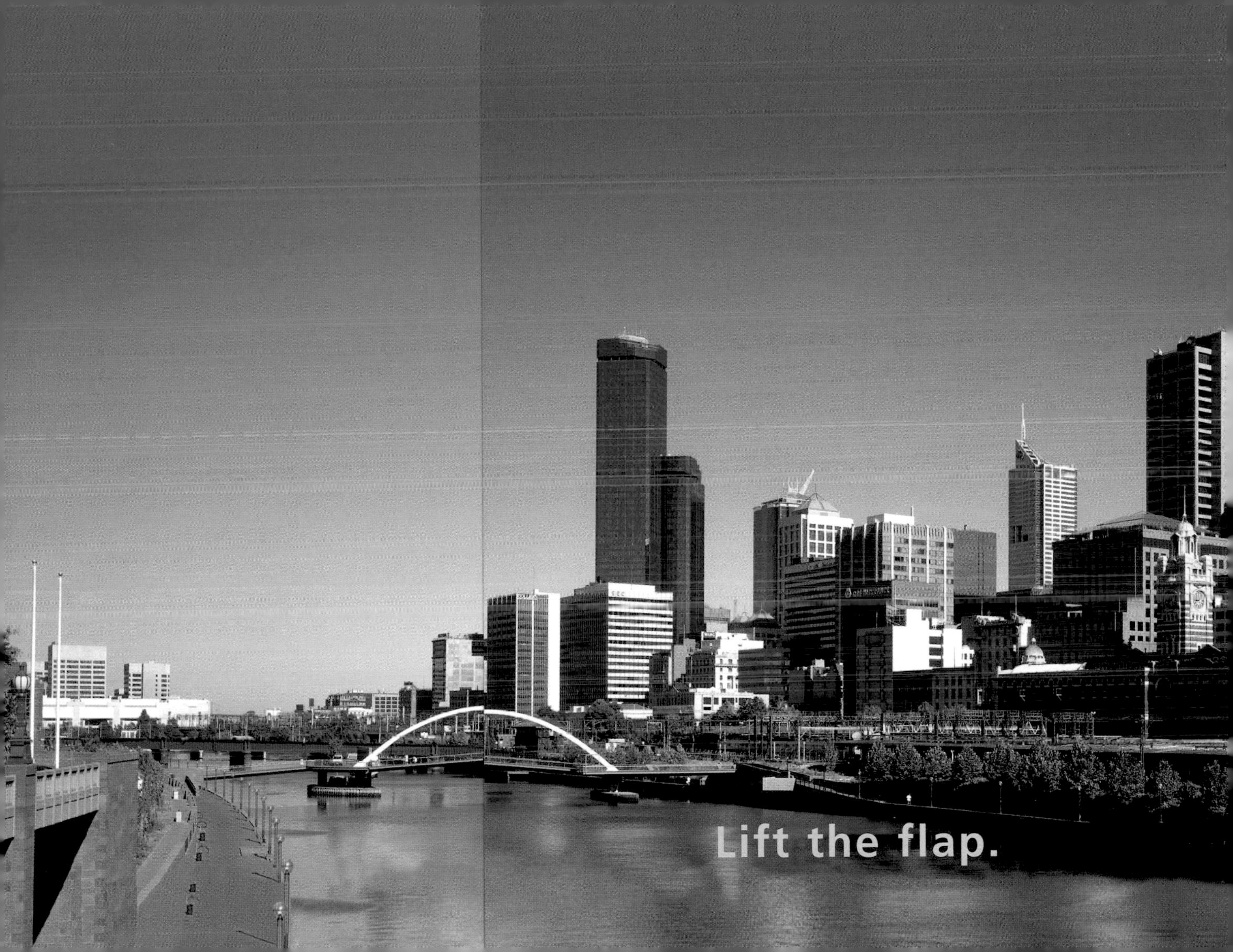
Lift the flap.

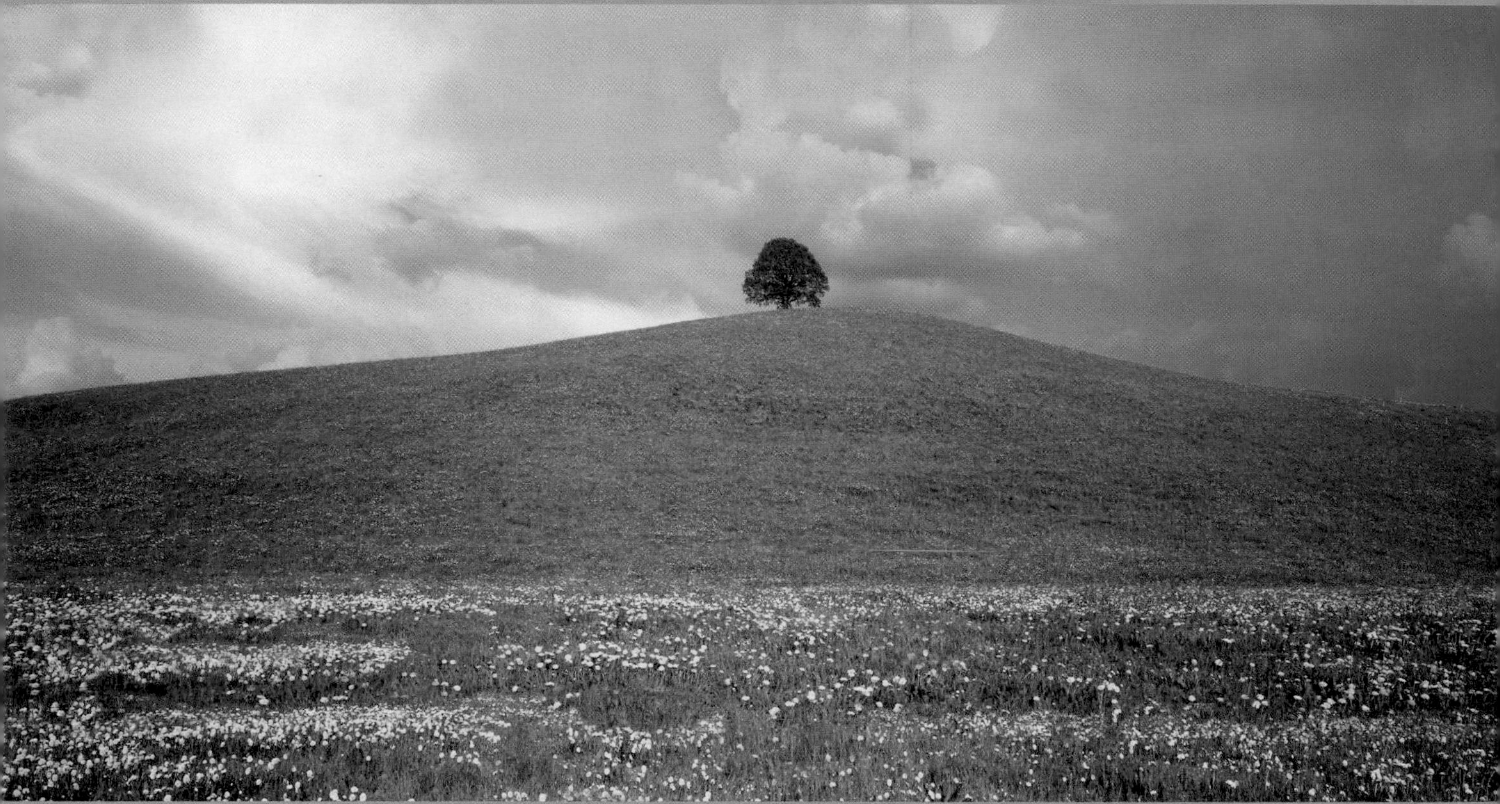

A hill is **big**.

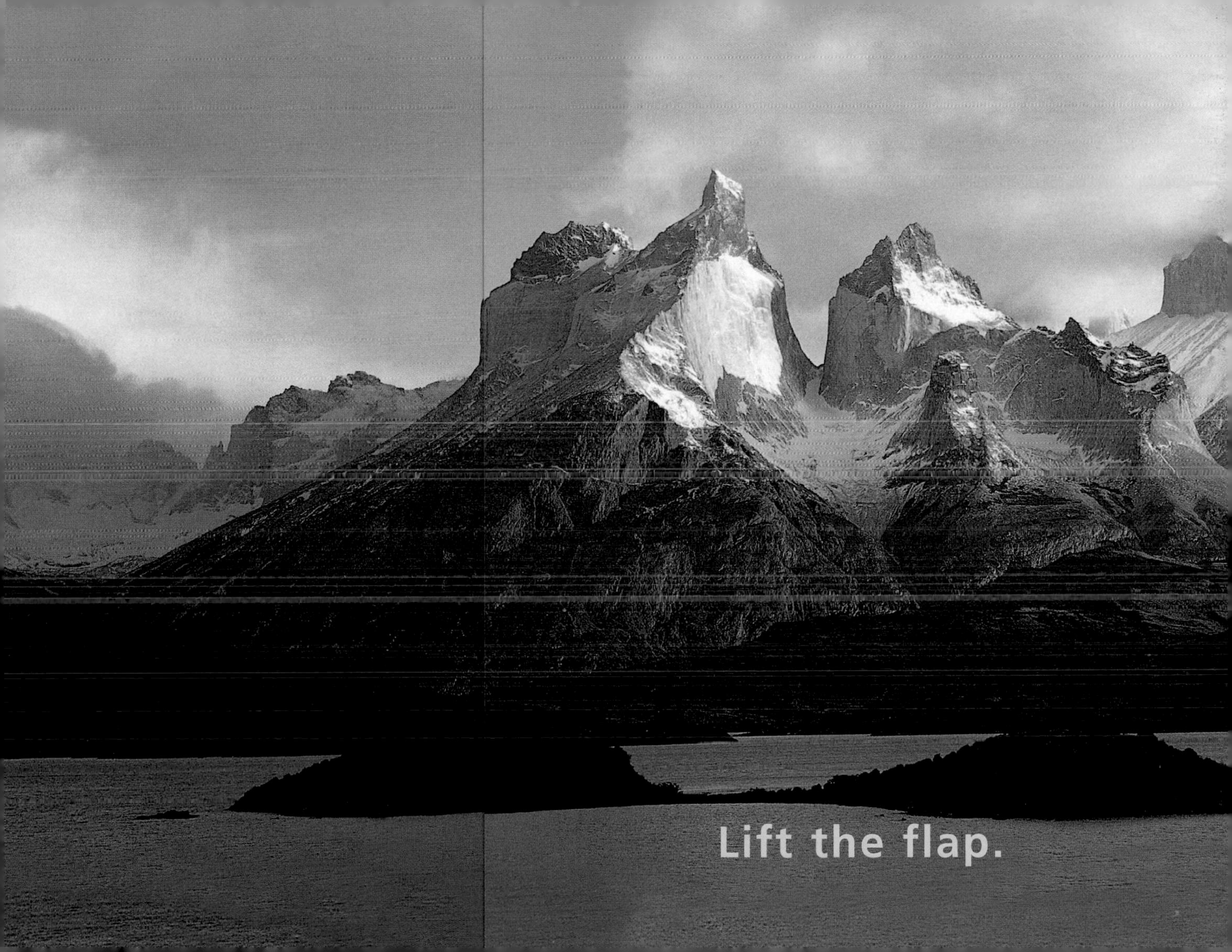
Lift the flap.

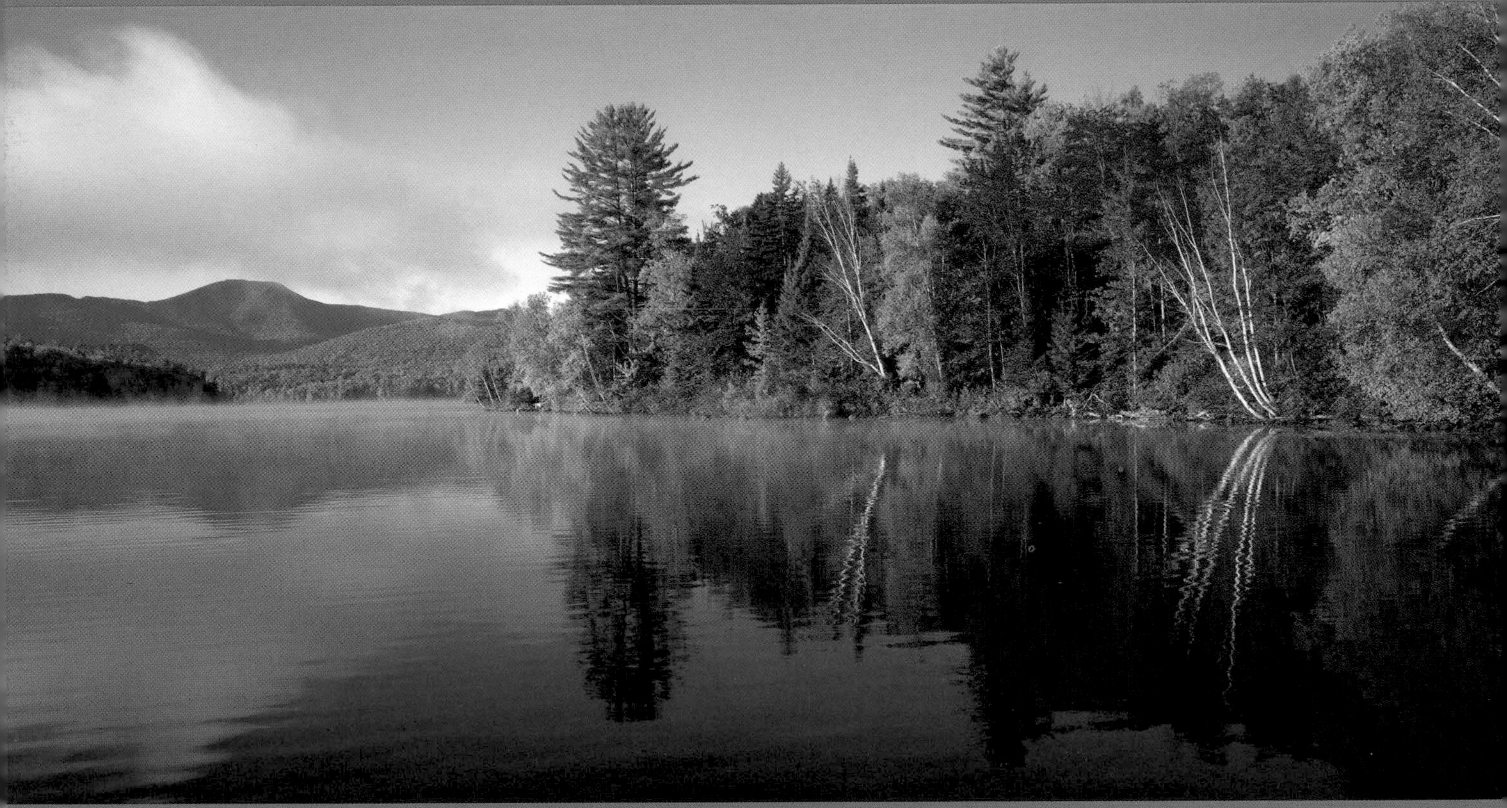

A lake is **big**.

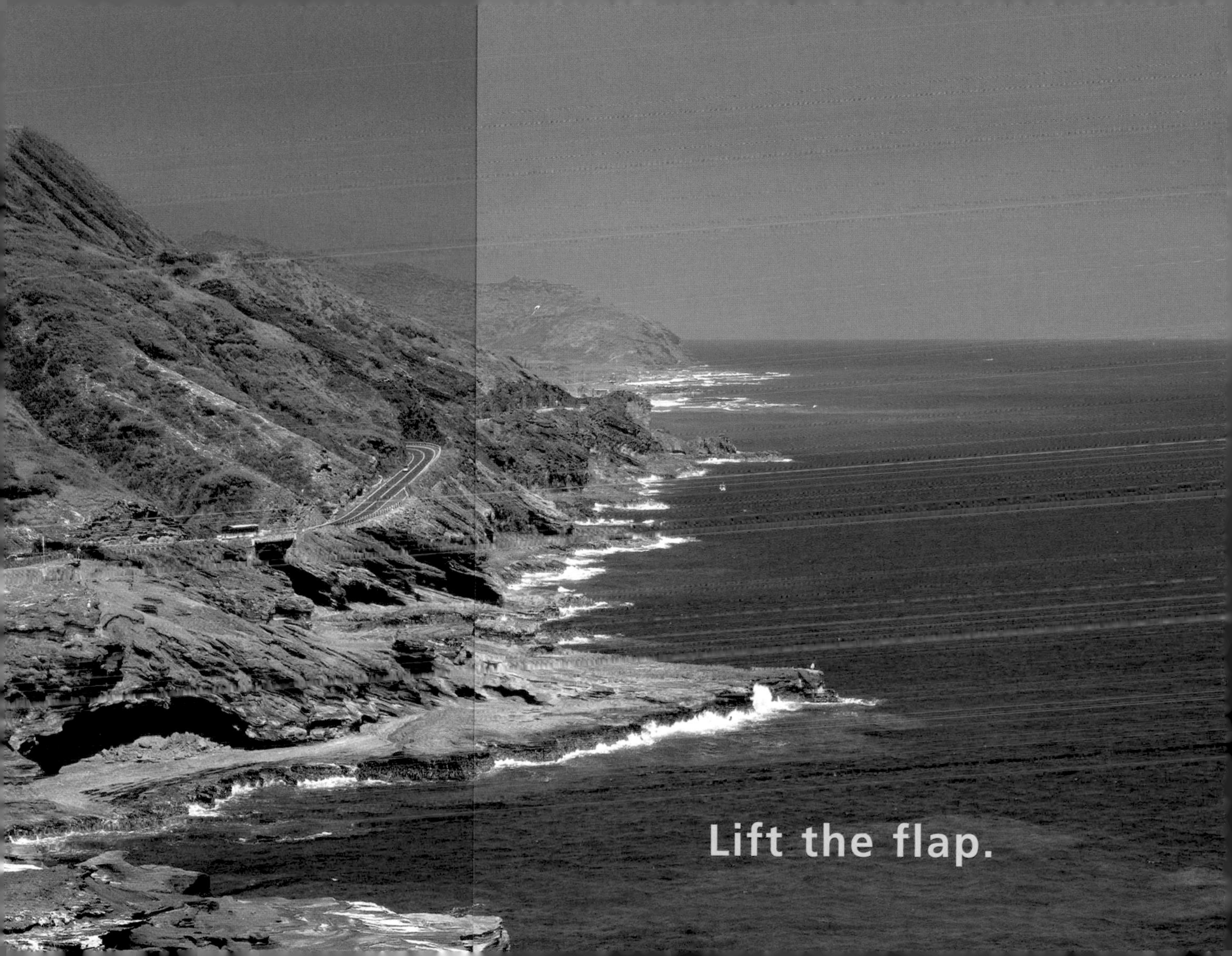

Lift the flap.

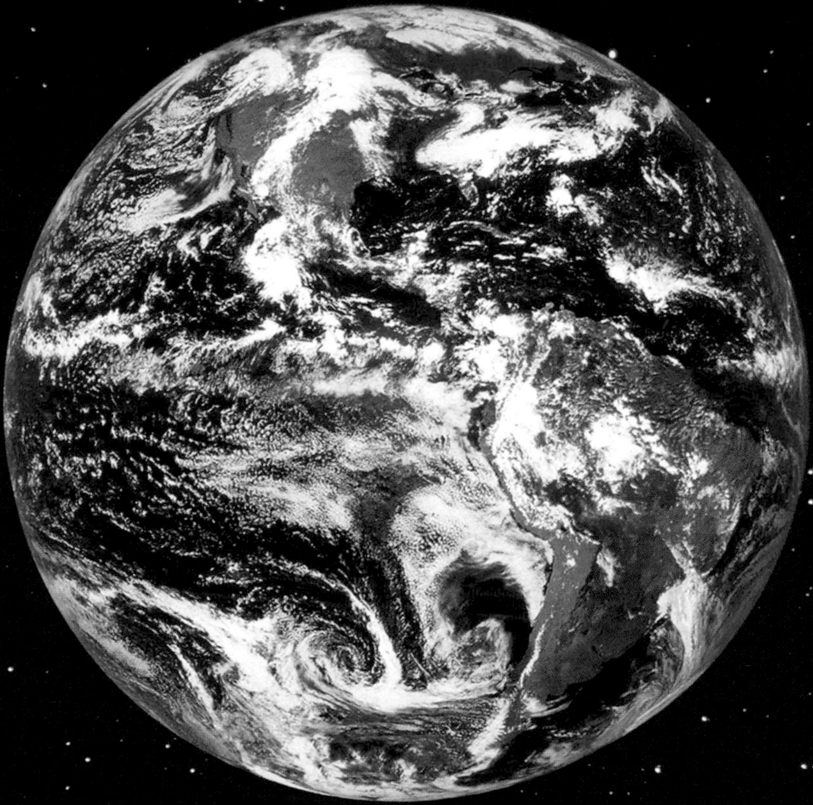

Our world is **big**.